Stars

Published by Waxwing

24.03.2017 ©

ISBN 978 1 922220 26 4

You See Stars Everywhere

By Bakthi Ross

ILLUSTRATED BY BAKTHI ROSS

You see stars in the sky.
You see stars on land.
A star fish under the sea do
not swim like a fish.

A star could have five, six, seven, eight or more points.

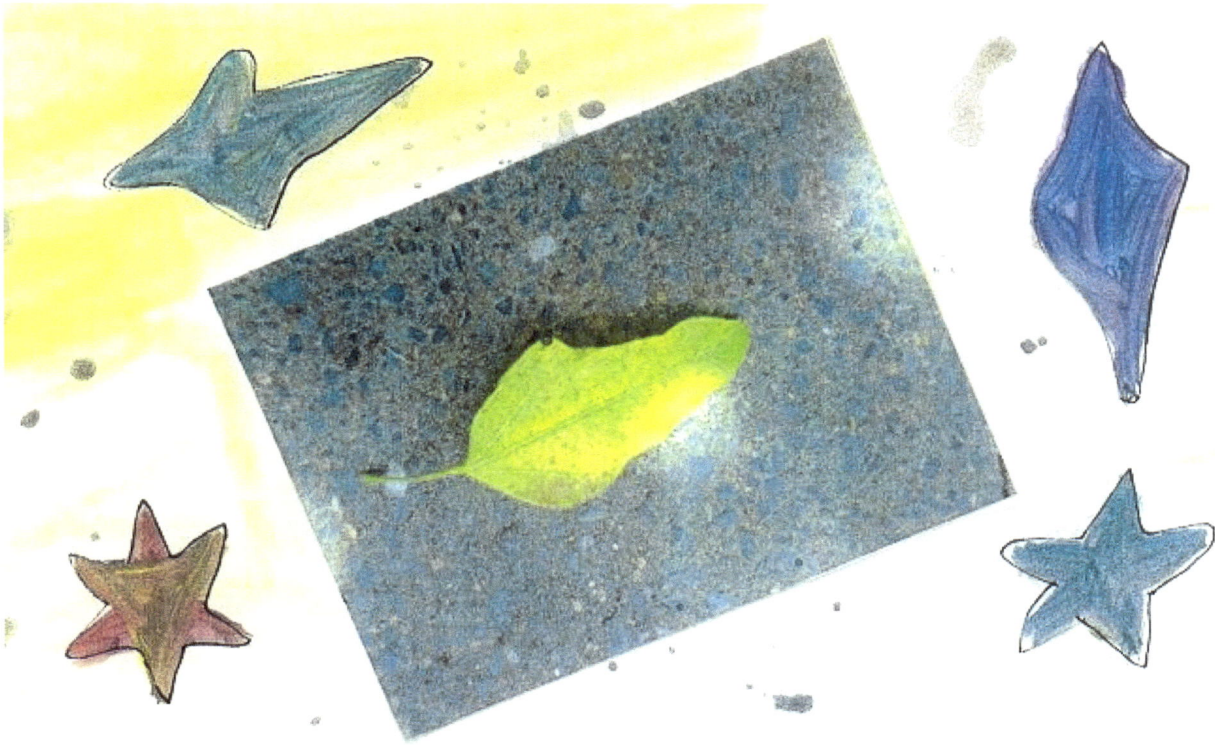

When leaves and flowers
form they have parts of the
star-shape.

A leaf with three parts of the star-shape.

A leaf with five parts of a star-shape.

A leaf with seven parts of a star-shape.

A star break is how light breaks
in rays and beams to form a
star-shape in pressure. Light
breaks like a star-shape to
make pointy corners on leaves.

Leaves and flowers rotates and break like a circle of stars.

Stars upon stars make the
branch look like a tree of stars.

Stars of leaves and flowers
make a family of stars.

Layers of stars covers the sky.
Layers of stars covers the land.
Layers of stars covers the sea.

When I see stars I see light. The sun, a star for many, shining upon us. A life giving light.

Chain of stars moves towards the light.

Circles of stars make flowers
and leaves cluster.

Without pressure flowers would
not break open like a star to see
the sky.

A star is a place you land, you stand, and you smile.
Star breaks in all life forms.
Everything breaks and forms like the stars.

www.ingramcontent.com/pod-product-compliance
Lightning Source LLC
Chambersburg PA
CBHW060827270326
41931CB00002B/88